# DIGITAL SUNSET
# DIGITAL SUNRISE
a vaporwave love story

by kaixxa

"Do not think before you answer: who do you love?"
— Austin Moran

inspired by
colors + internet + technology + love

i love you, Davo.

part 1: poems
part 2: a vaporwave love story
part 3: more poems

*table of contents

part 1

*poems

sprint towards the sunrise

let the music wash over you like a blanket of ocean

a bus called 94 sun valley

They tell me of strange lands where there are bright yellow fruits

i let the haunting vocals soak my soul pearl iridescent

i let the haunting vocals fry my soul crispy

boy what that soul do

i took his hand and we dived into the digital sunset

it was all neon grey and photoshop pink

it was all chemical burn

and all bending of time and space

i said let's drown in the digital ocean
he said sure why not

part 2:
DIGITAL SUNSET
DIGITAL SUNRISE

*a vaporwave love story

this story is an outlet for my misplaced emotions for someone with whom i have what i believe is called budding love with who is perpetually one thousand miles away from me

it's a vaporwave love story

there was a digital ocean all hot pink pixels and all bright
orange gradient

i drew my lover on a boat in photoshop and off we went
some might call it an adventure i would call it a nightmare

big wave then
all glitch screams and all hands on deck

i should have used the pen tool in illustrator
to make us some planks
i should have used vector art
to make us a sail

because we resized the boat in photoshop
and now it has leaks

big gaping gashes in the bow, or the stern, or the cross bow,
i'm not really sure because i don't know anything about boats

i'm just a digital citizen, all addict and all hints of kilobytes
in my thin veins

eyes pale from never going outside
skin dry from never looking at a face like his
what is
fresh air

chapter 2

so anyway he and i are on this boat, right
it's storming and i'm not sure where we're going
we make out for a bit and then we get down to business
the business of saving ourselves

i drink some of the water and it's sweet like cola,
scratchy on the way down my throat

i suppose i should mention that he's not my lover
just a crush
just a pen pal
just a hope
just a wisp of a hope

we've never even kissed
or held hands
just locked eyes over a cup of coffee
once

so anyway there are leaks in the boat and they are huge

the bright orange water from this digital ocean is vying to capsize us
the leaks are not leaks, they're gashes
big gaping holes in our souls
like the void after losing a loved one

the water rushes in like tiny tangerine rivers
yep, like tiny tangerine rivers
it's like we're in a sunkist commercial gone wrong

i try to plug them with the heel of my foot
when suddenly Davo pokes me in the back
and points to the sky
the clear, gray sky

there appears a giant floating Internet Explorer icon in the distance

all blue and all giant "e"
we frantically paddle towards it

perhaps it is our savior perhaps it is our satan but we trudge on

perhaps we are supposed to learn some crucial life lesson or
listen to its cautionary tale i'm not entirely sure

who really knows

somehow Davo my partner in avoiding the watery grave clicks
the icon with his subconscious mind
Davo is pretty chill, I wrote a poem about him.*

we wait.

*the poem about him is after this
short story

we get the feeling that it will take forever to load
because it only appears as sliver thin bars of glitcheryness

one
bar
at
a
time

an error screen appears saying
error 455 you cannot leave
error 455 you cannot leave

so we wait for what seems like an eternity
i believe it was an eternity
i believe it was literally an actual eternity
an eternity complete with one thousand lives born and lived
and died

The sentient Internet Explorer icon walks up with cartoon eyes and a high-pitched voice.

He comments in a highly verbose, self-aware manner:

"I'm here to impart a highly moral lesson in order to cause a paradigm shift in your life. How may I guide you in extremely obtuse language in a parable sort of format that will send you on a convoluted but epic quest to "find yourselves" and ultimately grow and become better people?"

Davion says, "I'll pass."

"Very well then."

The sky cracked at its centre and bars of bright pink broken
screen seemed to create a sunset, a digital sunset

there was a sense of violence and urgency in the air

we keep paddling haphazardly with a makeshift oar made of
a discarded windows 98 search bar.

I kiss Davo on the cheek
we're gonna live
we're gonna make it baby
he retorts: "We don't have time for this."

All I can think of is, wow, he didn't push me away. Even
though this is my own fantasy, I'm still surprised.

A sinister, clown-like theme song blares from the horizon and Clippy the animated Microsoft Office assistant appears.

He has a permanent grin, with bugged out eyes replete with deep black sunglasses, which is a new look for him. He is grasping a palm tree in his gloved hand.

Recall that Clippy is a sentient paper clip.

"Well look-y here." He regards in his chipper yet sinister yet incredibly servile and helpful tone.

"We got two love birds here. Y'all an item?"

I mutter, "I wish."

Davion turns red and retorts, "Who is this paper clip fool?"

I whisper: "He's that dude from old school Microsoft Word."

"Y'all need to get up out of here." Clippy picks his teeth with a toothpick that appears from nowhere, which was surprisingly unsettling, considering that he doesn't have teeth.

"Why?"

"Because trouble's afoot. There's a virus around here and if you don't x out the window, it's gonna steal your human souls or render them unusable or something

"What window?"

He sighed.

"Don't you realize you're in a square of orange pixels in the color palette of a giant MS Paint window?"

"What???"

"Yeah. For real."

"We're trapped in a computer?

"Bingo. You got it. Bet."

"So, all of this" — I gestured to the sea of orange — "isn't real?"

The ocean stretched in every direction; the horizon
was endless. The sky was the dark, chilling, and gray
realization that we were floating in yes, you guessed it,
a Windows 98 window.

Clippy retorted, "I mean, is anything really "real"?

Davo nodded and said, "True. You right, you right,
my paperclip pal."

I suppose it had been kind of strange how the water
had scratched my throat when I tasted it.

Because it wasn't water, it was pixels.
—Pixels taste sweet, if you were ever wondering.

"So, if we're at the bottom of an MS Paint window, there are 27 more oceans, right? Blue, purple, yellow, cerulean?"

Clips nodded.

"And if we don't cap this virus or whatever,
our human souls are lost to damnation or
limbo or erasure or something like that?"

He again nodded.

Not sure how I am so certain that Clippy is a he,
but let's go with it.

"But why are we here?"

"No one really knows why, we tribunal of ancient
Windows 98 icons only know the how.

You were downloaded from your previous
human lives and summoned here, to this vast
— well, little — square ocean of pixels."

I said, "I thought the Internet Explorer thing said that there was no parable, no impetus, no moral lesson to be learned?"

"He lied."

I tried to breathe. I tried to meditate. I tried to think of happy thoughts. I thought of how maybe one day Davion and I would live out our artistic lives together somewhere in sunny Southern California replete with in-home art studios, organic açaí bowls, inside jokes, and endless laughs. We wouldn't have any kids, we'd start a zine. A long-standing yet niche and artsy kind of zine. For the culture, not the profit. But this line of thinking was wholly unhelpful in this moment.

For a few seconds, we paused and considered all that the all-knowing and all-powerful Clippy — who gave off petty deity vibes — had said.

Davo broke the silence, the silence that was pregnant with confusion:

"So what are we supposed to do now?"

Clippy begrudgingly said he could use his body as a slingshot to catapult us to the x — or to a better view, so we could find the x and save ourselves.

"Well —" we stared at each other — "We really don't have a choice, do we?"

"No, not really."

Davo shrugged.

I took his hand.

After very little planning, Clippy shot us into the sky with his sentient paperclip parts which were unsettlingly and disturbingly damp. I didn't ask any questions, I didn't want to know.

We were catapulted up up up into an emotional and metaphysical limbo

Primarily because I still wasn't sure if Davo was down for me or not.

But that's besides the point, because I had to put those thoughts aside and focus at the task at hand.

I saw the little pats of color all neatly squared up as
a palette at the bottom of the MS Paint window and i
had some life altering, life affirming thought about the
frailty of life and the beauty of — you know I can't
really remember what the insight was anymore.

Everything went dark and i discovered that one of my
hands was grasping Davo's fingers tightly. He had
such beautiful hands. Artist's hands. Well manicured,
clean nails and — I'm getting off track here.

— the other hand was holding what i can only describe
as a tail.

A very spiky tail.

I dared to look ahead and the creature who possessed
the tail moved like a snake weaving to and fro,
weaving back and forth.

Flashes of red and yellow and green and blue told me
all that I needed to know.

We were riding on the proverbial back of the Windows
98 flag.

— the image burned dead alive into the bas relief
consciousness of any human living in the modern
world.

I heard a metallic groan and the darkness around us lit
up in a blinding flash.

i smelled smoke and the groan expanded into the

dun dun da dun dunnnnnnn

of the Windows 98 startup sound

According to Wikipedia, "the startup sound for Windows 98
was composed by Microsoft sound engineer Ken Kato,
who considered it to be a 'tough act to follow.'"

Our ears started to bleed because it glitched and scratched
like a record.

da dun dunNnNnNNNnnNnNNNNNn

it went on for an eternity,

a literal actual eternity

an eternity complete with one thousand lives lived and died

by then our skin and organs had boiled, we were inside
out. yes, our innards had folded inside out of themselves,

my fingers to type this were now where my heart should be

and my heart was hanging exposed in this terrifying dark
digital chasm

but my heart was still with Davo

We were in the *corazón*, the heart of the virus, not sure why I threw a Spanish word in there, guess I'm still a bit mixed up or just trying to show off who knows

Somehow I could still talk to Davo even though my mouth was where my stomach should have been and my stomach was in my mouth's position, all folded and flapping.

And he could hear and understand me, because we just have such a good connection like that, a connection that transcends space, time, and the difference between a digital and physical existence.

Or maybe we were just tripping our balls — his balls,
my ovaries, to be anatomically correct — off.

Somehow the idea came to me to simply punch the corrupted, infected, omniscient Windows 98 icon slash virus in the throat, which for some reason seemed blasphemous as the icon kind of gave off slight Jehovah vibes,

and the idea was kind of unsettling and kind of disturbing
because it doesn't have a throat and it gave off a shrill
google scream but it worked and now we're free

I'm sure you want to know how and why and when and the *details*

but it really isn't important
it really isn't important at all

what's important is that
i told Davo i loved him
and he said no thanks

Dangerous be these artsy boys

*a poem about Davo

1
he was sacrosanct
practically sacrosanct

all watercolor skin
all india ink eyes

all bite and no bark

he was a quiet man
worked construction by day
made art / art school student by night

i loved him and he said
no thanks

2
all paintbrush fingers
all Michelangelo nose

all Caravaggio eyes
all acrylic soul

acrylic like chemical soul
but i thought it was oil
rich sweet if you inhale too much i'll kill you oil
fun fact
if you breathe too much oil paint it will kill you oil

all bright purple hair
on fire,
on fire.
two-strand twists never looked so good
too bad it was a lie

part 3

*more poems

perhaps it is our savior perhaps it is our satan but we trudge on

it was a dark, stormy night and
the pilot fought for that landing

"we are just consuming sun"
- after volen ck

the sun eaters
we are the sun eaters

arms dripping with gold paint
eyes blinded by gold leaf
hunger drips from our silver teeth
glowing gold worshippers

god help us ascend
god help us suicide beautiful

we are the sun soldiers, we soldier on
sun soldiers, sun solders
we carry on

we out here

"we out here tryna transcend the flesh"
-after post crunk

we out here tryna transcend the monotony

we out here tryna transcend the corpse

we out here tryna transcend

we out here tryin

we out here

ancient internet proverbs

AOL altar

Holy QWERTY Spirit

vaporwave hymns sung at an Internet church

open mic night idea: a man high on salvia sincerely believes that he is a glass of orange juice and is deathly afraid that his friends will drink him

such golden rays of ocean. such golden ocean of rays.

*after @lexitrobe22

tropicana lanes
waves of teal and orange

just another sunny day in southern california

just another somber day in southern california

it's not always sunny in southern california

just another day

without him

Published by:
poetry by kaixxa

ISBN: 978-0-578-42218-3

For press and business inquiries, contact the author:
E-mail: theemprischannel@gmail.com

Acknowledgments to the artist who created the cover art:
I have been searching for you and will give you 3% of any
profits that I earn from this collection of poetry and prose.

about the author

i am a post-post-modernist poet living in los angeles, california.

follow me on social media for daily poems:
https://www.instagram.com/poetrybykaixxa
https://twitter.com/kaixxa_

Manufactured by Amazon.ca
Bolton, ON

14211534R00083